HAUNTED WORLD

FAMOUS GHOST STORIES OF EUROPE

by Matt Chandler

CAPSTONE PRESS
a capstone imprint

Edge Books are published by Capstone Press,
1710 Roe Crest Drive, North Mankato, Minnesota 56003
www.mycapstone.com

Copyright © 2019 by Capstone Press, a Capstone imprint. All rights reserved.
No part of this publication may be reproduced in whole or in part, or stored
in a retrieval system, or transmitted in any form or by any means, electronic,
mechanical, photocopying, recording, or otherwise, without written permission
of the publisher.

Library of Congress Cataloging-in-Publication Data
Library of Congress Cataloging-in-Publication Data is available on the Library
of Congress website.
ISBN: 978-1-5435-2592-2 (hardcover)
ISBN: 978-1-5435-2596-0 (paperback)
ISBN: 978-1-5435-2600-4 (eBook PDF)

Editorial Credits
Carrie Braulick Sheely, editor; Kyle Grenz, designer; Svetlana Zhurkin,
media researcher; Kathy McColley, production specialist

Photo Credits
Dreamstime: Sue Martin, 5, 7; Getty Images: Marco Di Lauro, 16, Paris Match/
Manuel Litran, 27, The LIFE Picture Collection/Pictures Inc./Time Life Pictures,
13; iStockphoto: duncan1890, 22, Philartphace, 25; Newscom: akg-images/A.F.
Kersting, 12, Heritage Images/The Print Collector, 21, NI Syndication/Gill Allen,
19, Westend61 GmbH/Harald Nachtmann, 8–9; Shutterstock: Aleksey Stemmer,
10–11, alredosaz, 24, Benoit Daoust, 17, Dmitry Tereshchenko, cover (front),
Guillermo Pis Gonzalez, cover (back), Nanisimova, 14, observe.co, 26, Olga_i, 23
(top), paula french, 20, Peter Etchells, 28, Pyty (map), 5, 8, 12, 14, 16, 18, 20, 24, 26,
28, 29, Scharfsinn, 15, Songkran Wannatat, 23 (bottom), Stas Guk, 4

Design Elements by Shutterstock

TABLE OF CONTENTS

ARE YOU SCARED YET?........4
ANCIENT RAM INN..............5
WOLFSEGG CASTLE............8
RAYNHAM HALL................12
AKERSHUS FORTRESS.........14
POVEGLIA ISLAND.............16
LANGHAM HOTEL..............18
TOWER OF LONDON...........20
EDINBURGH CASTLE..........24
THE PARIS CATACOMBS......26
RUTHIN CASTLE HOTEL......28

    MAP.............29
    GLOSSARY........30
    READ MORE.......31
    INTERNET SITES...31
    INDEX..........32

Are You Scared Yet?

What's the scariest ghost story you've ever heard? Maybe it was a tale about a local house or hotel. People tell stories about creepy **haunted** places around the world. Some of the world's most terrifying ghost stories are from Europe. People have reported seeing headless ghosts haunting old castles. Hotel guests say they've been touched by **spirits** from beyond the grave. These ghostly encounters often happen in places where many people have died. Are the ghost stories fact or fiction? Decide for yourself after you explore some of the most well-known haunted places in Europe.

Thinking about visiting the Paris Catacombs in France?

You might change your mind after learning about their reported hauntings!

Ancient Ram Inn

LOCATION: GLOUCESTERSHIRE, ENGLAND

The Ancient Ram Inn is said to be one of the most haunted inns in England. The ghost of Mary Gibbons is especially well known there. In the 1500s witch hunts became common in Europe. Locals sometimes tied suspected witches to stakes and burned them to death. Gibbons had been accused of being a witch. She tried to hide at the inn, but she was found and put to death.

Today Gibbons' ghost is said to haunt the "Witch's Room." People have reported seeing dark shapes moving in the room. Ghost hunters have claimed to hear the voice of Mary's ghost there. They say her spirit was heard on tape answering questions.

haunted—having mysterious events happen often, possibly due to visits from ghosts

spirit—a ghost

For decades the inn has been a private residence, but that hasn't stopped the creepy reports from coming. Owner John Humphries claims to have regular run-ins with the dead. Humphries told a tale of being dragged from his bed by what he called a demon force on his first night in the home.

Visitors to the inn continue to report unexplained experiences. Ghost hunters say they've captured the voice of a male ghost using **EVP** equipment. Visitors have reported **orbs** in photographs they took at the inn. **Paranormal** experts believe orbs could be a sign that ghosts were present when a photo was taken.

EVP—sounds or voices heard during electronic recordings that can't be explained; EVP stands for electronic voice phenomenon

orb—a glowing ball of light that sometimes appears in photographs taken at reportedly haunted locations

paranormal—having to do with an event that has no scientific explanation

Why are all these creepy happenings being reported at the inn? Some paranormal experts say a ley line is to blame. A ley line is said to form when two landforms or structures are connected by a straight line. Some people believe these lines allow energy and ghosts to travel freely between the two places. The inn sits on the intersection of two ley lines connecting it to Stonehenge. Stonehenge is one of the most famous tourist attractions in England. The stone structure and its burial ground date back more than 5,000 years. Could the spirits of those buried at Stonehenge be traveling the ley line to the Ancient Ram Inn?

the Ancient Ram Inn

Wolfsegg Castle

LOCATION: WOLFSEGG, GERMANY

Wolfsegg, Germany, is home to an 800-year-old castle with a mysterious past. For many years visitors have reported encounters with a spirit known as the "Woman in White." Many people think the ghost is the spirit of Klara von Helfenstein. She was murdered in the castle in the 1500s.

    Some of the creepiest reports don't even include ghost sightings. Visitors have reported feeling unexplained sadness near the room where Klara died. They also have reported feeling pulled to the room by an invisible force.

    The Woman in White may be spooky, but locals say the true terror of Wolfsegg is found in the dark woods behind the castle. Daring visitors who go there can find The Hole. Locals say this cave holds many dark secrets. For hundreds of years, people have reported strange, terrifying noises coming from inside. Moaning and wailing sounds are said to pierce the night, shattering the silence of the forest.

A legend says the terror of The Hole dates back to the disappearance of a man named Georg Moller. Klara von Helfenstein had hired Moller for protection while her husband was away. Soon after Klara was murdered, he went walking in the woods behind the castle. He was never seen again. Locals say that since then, others who have dared to go exploring in the woods have also vanished.

FACT
Some people say the two men who murdered Klara von Helfenstein also haunt the castle.

In the 1920s scientists went into The Hole to try to find out more about what was happening there. They found hundreds of animal bones. Are animals making the wails and moans coming from the darkness or is something far creepier responsible?

Raynham Hall

LOCATION: NORFOLK, ENGLAND

Raynham Hall is said to be haunted by the ghost of a woman who has been dead for nearly 300 years. Lady Dorothy Walpole lived there with her husband, Charles Townshend, in the early 1700s. Townshend became angry with her and locked her away in a tower on the property. Unable to escape, she died sick and alone. More than 100 years after her death, a witness first reported seeing her ghost. It was the first of many reports.

Country Life's 1936 *Raynham Hall* photo

Witnesses say the ghost of Lady Dorothy Walpole floats through the halls of the **estate**. The ghost has earned the nickname "The Brown Lady" because she is always wearing a long, brown dress. Some people say the spooky spirit has a glowing face but empty sockets where her eyes should be. Witnesses have described her as having a crazed smile on her face. Sometimes she carries a lantern.

In 1936 a photographer working for *Country Life* magazine was at Raynham Hall taking pictures. On the grand staircase, he photographed what he believed was the ghost of Lady Walpole. The magazine published the image. Soon thousands of visitors came to the estate hoping to meet its most famous ghost.

FACT

Experts have proven many of the "ghosts" in photographs to be shadows. Reflections on the lens or other lighting in a room can cause these mysterious shadows.

estate—a large area of land, usually with a house on it

13

Akershus Fortress

LOCATION: OSLO, NORWAY

Like many haunted places, Akershus Fortress has a violent past. King Hakon V ordered the castle built in 1299. It overlooked the Oslo Fjord. Its position allowed the military to see enemies coming toward Oslo across the water. It later was a military fortress and a prison. Prison authorities sometimes beat and killed prisoners there. Nazis later used the site during World War II (1939-1945) to carry out enemy **executions**. With so much death and misery at Akershus comes many spooky tales.

execution—putting someone to death

The ghost of a woman named Mantelgeisten reportedly lives in the fortress. Visitors have reported seeing her dressed in a long, flowing robe. Many witnesses say she has no face.

The most famous ghost said to haunt Akershus isn't the spirit of a human. A horrible ghost dog named Malcanisen reportedly guards the entrance to the fortress. It is said that anyone who encounters the creepy canine ghost will suffer a horrible death within three months.

According to legend a commander of the Norwegian Armed Forces ordered that a dog be buried alive at the fortress' front gates hundreds of years ago. The commander believed the ghost of the dog would provide protection for the men inside. He may have been right. Over the years, military forces have attacked Akershus many times, but it was never captured by force.

> **FACT**
>
> In English *Malcanisen* means "evil dog."

Poveglia Island

LOCATION: ITALY

In the mid-1300s, a terrible disease known as the Black Death struck Europe. The disease killed about one-third of Europe's population. Many cities used islands and other isolated places to **quarantine** the sick. Poveglia Island near Venice, Italy, was home to thousands of sick Italians. Most died slow, painful deaths. Workers also transported tens of thousands of dead bodies to the island while the plague was spreading. It's said that half of the island contains human remains. It may come as no surprise that the island has long been the site of ghostly occurrences.

quarantine—to keep a person, animal, or plant away from others to stop a disease from spreading

FACT

The Italian government owned Poveglia Island until 2014. Before selling it, the government forbid visitors to go there. But brave souls still snuck onto the island to try to meet the spirits of the dead.

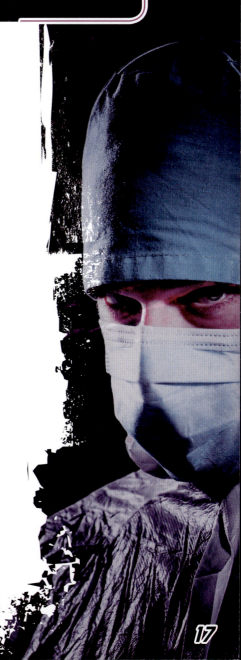

One of the most mysterious ghostly tales involves an old bell tower on the island. In the late 1800s, a **psychiatric** hospital was on the island. Legend says one doctor was known for conducting many cruel experiments on the patients. He threw himself to his death from the bell tower. Today locals living on the mainland claim to hear the bell chime. There's just one problem—the bell is no longer there! Many locals are convinced it is the dead man ringing the bell from beyond the grave.

One local Italian man reports spending 15 nights on the island in the mid-1900s. He reported seeing the ghost of a doctor. The man claims the doctor pushed him and that the ghost could make objects fly around him.

psychiatric—related to a branch of medicine that studies the mind, emotions, and behavior

Langham Hotel

LOCATION: LONDON, ENGLAND

Sometimes ghosts in hotels seem to bother guests in certain rooms. This is true of London's Langham Hotel. If ghost hunters visit the hotel, they often request to stay in room 333. Witnesses have reported several ghosts in the room, including a doctor with blank eyes. The doctor is said to have killed his wife and himself in the room while on their honeymoon. Visitors also have reported seeing the ghost of a German prince dressed in his military uniform. The noble ghost passes through solid walls and doors. The prince is believed to have jumped to his death from an upper floor of the hotel.

In 1973 a guest staying in room 333 reported a terrifying encounter with a white orb. The ball of light transformed into a ghostly man wearing Victorian clothing right in front of his eyes! The guest fled the room in terror. The ghost has been seen several times since.

FACT

One woman staying in room 333 said a ghost had violently shook her bed. She fled the hotel in the middle of the night.

Despite these spine-tingling tales, Room 333 has become a popular tourist attraction. Ghost hunters may pay more than $650 to spend the night.

Tower of London

LOCATION: LONDON, ENGLAND

The Tower of London is more than 1,000 years old. It has a bloody history. Many people have been murdered there. One of the most mysterious tales of murder involves two young princes. In 1674 workers tearing down an old staircase in the tower uncovered two small skeletons. Nearly 200 years earlier, two young princes were killed on the grounds. Historians believe the skeletons unearthed were those of the young boys.

Today the mystery of who killed the boys and why remains. Many people suspect the boys' uncle Richard had them killed to have a better chance at becoming king.

King Charles II ordered a royal burial of the bodies at Westminster Abbey to honor them. But although the remains of the bodies are now gone, their spirits may have stayed in the tower. Many witnesses have reported seeing ghosts of the princes over the years. They are dressed in white and often hold hands, as if trying to protect each other.

The wife of one of the tower's guards once saw the ghosts dressed in white nightshirts. They held each other in front of a fireplace. When the woman told her husband, he laughed. He pointed out there was no fireplace in the room. Little did he know that behind the wall was a fireplace that had been covered up!

> **FACT**
> The Tower of London was built as a royal palace. It was then used as a prison for several hundred years. Today ghost sightings include both prisoners and royalty.

The Tower of London has also been the site of more than 100 executions. Visitors have reported seeing headless ghosts roaming throughout the tower since the 1300s. The most famous is the spirit of Queen Anne Boleyn, wife of King Henry VIII. She was killed in the tower in 1536. Many people have spotted her ghost wandering the grounds in a bloody dress. Witnesses often see her near the Queen's House.

Queen Anne Boleyn

Yet the dead that are said to haunt the Tower of London aren't limited to human form. One story says a guard was on patrol in 1815 when he saw smoke coming from Martin Tower. The smoky mist soon took the form of an enormous bear. The guard tried to stab the animal with his bayonet. His weapon passed right through the bear and stuck in the door. After reporting the event, the guard went into shock. He never recovered and died two days later.

Edinburgh Castle

LOCATION:
EDINBURGH, SCOTLAND

Many people consider Edinburgh Castle one of the most haunted places in Scotland. Witnesses have reported many ghostly encounters in the castle's maze of underground tunnels. Those who dare to go in them may meet up with a ghost playing the bagpipes. Legend says the man was sent to explore the underground tunnels after they were first discovered. The man brought his bagpipes and played them as he walked so that the people above could track his movement. Suddenly, the music stopped and there was silence. Those in the castle quickly formed a search party and went after the piper. But they never found him, his body, or his bagpipes.

FACT

In 2001 a team of researchers sent almost 250 people into the castle without telling them any of its haunted history. Many people reported paranormal events. Most of the reports came from areas with a history of hauntings.

If a musical ghost isn't scary enough, castle visitors have reported many other frightening experiences. People have reported seeing ghosts of soldiers. Some were said to make physical contact with the terrified witnesses. One visitor reported being touched on the face by an unseen hand. Others have felt a tugging on their clothes from behind. When they quickly turned around, there was no one there—at least no one living!

Haunted Harmonies

Do you love music? Ghosts might too. People have reported ghosts playing pianos in hotels, banjos in prisons, and drums in castles. Why? Some people believe the answer is very simple. Music makes people happy. You might dance, sing, and smile when you hear a favorite song. Maybe the spirits of the dead seek out the things that made them happy in life, including music.

The Paris Catacombs

LOCATION: PARIS, FRANCE

Paris is known as the City of Love. Many couples travel to Paris on their honeymoons or for other special occasions. But as couples stroll the streets, the bones of 6 million people lie underneath them!

In the late 1700s people in Paris were running out of room to bury their dead. The government decided to move millions of bodies underground into a series of tunnels called catacombs. With all of these bones under Paris, it may come as no surprise that the Paris Catacombs are legendary for ghost stories.

catacomb—an underground cemetery, usually with tunnels and rooms

FACT

Visitors to the catacombs are searched when they come back up from the underground tombs. This became necessary after many visitors were caught stealing bones of the dead.

People have reported seeing ghosts and experiencing unexplained changes in temperature in the tunnels for many years. Some people think extreme temperature changes are a sign of ghost activity. Witnesses have claimed the skulls lining the walls came to life, moving as if watching them. Other tourists have reported hearing soft voices calling out to them from the walls of bones. Even with terrifying tales such as these, the Paris Catacombs remain a popular tourist attraction.

Ghostly Tourists

The Paris Catacombs cover nearly 200 miles (322 kilometers) underground. Many visitors have gotten lost in these dark, winding tunnels. Deaths are rare in the catacombs. But when they do occur, they tend to get a lot of attention. The most famous disappearance involves Frenchman Philibert Aspairt. He went into the catacombs in 1793 and never returned. Visitors found his remains in 1804 near one of the exits. He appeared to have almost made it out of the deadly maze. Could his be among the spirits that haunt the passageways today?

Ruthin Castle Hotel

LOCATION: RUTHIN, WALES

Paranormal researchers say ghosts often haunt the places where they died. That might explain the many reported sightings of "The Grey Lady" at Ruthin Castle Hotel. Legend says she is the ghost of a woman who was sentenced to death there. Castle workers buried her on the property hundreds of years ago.

Today the castle is a luxury hotel. Visitors who have seen the Grey Lady say she is dressed completely in gray. She floats quietly throughout the castle and outside. Many tourists claim to have captured photographs of the mysterious spirit.

FACT

The Grey Lady was buried just outside the entrance to the castle. Her grave is still visible today.

The Grey Lady isn't the only ghost reported at Ruthin Castle. People have reported sightings of a ghostly knight in full armor as well as the ghost of a small child. Some of these ghosts may even be able to interact with the living. People have reported being touched, grabbed, or even held down by unseen forces.

Haunted Places of Europe

1. Ancient Ram Inn · Gloucestershire, England
2. Wolfsegg Castle · Wolfsegg, Germany
3. Raynham Hall · Norfolk, England
4. Akershus Fortress · Oslo, Norway
5. Poveglia Island · Venetian Lagoon, Italy
6. Langham Hotel · London, England
7. Tower of London · London, England
8. Edinburgh Castle · Edinburgh, Scotland
9. Paris Catacombs · Paris, France
10. Ruthin Castle Hotel · Ruthin, Wales
11. Leap Castle · County Offaly, Ireland
12. Houska Castle · Blatce, Czech Republic
13. The Kremlin · Moscow, Russia
14. Banffy Castle · Bontida, Romania
15. Witches' Pond · Boldu-Creteasca Forest, Romania
16. The Borgvattnet Vicarage · Borgvattnet, Sweden

GLOSSARY

catacomb (CAT-uh-kohm)—an underground cemetery, usually with tunnels and rooms

estate (e-STAYT)—a large area of land, usually with a house on it

EVP—sounds or voices heard during electronic recordings that can't be explained; EVP stands for electronic voice phenomenon

execution (ek-si-KYOO-shuhn)—putting someone to death

haunted (HAWN-ted)—having mysterious events happen often, possibly due to visits from ghosts

orb (ORB)—a glowing ball of light that sometimes appears in photographs taken at reportedly haunted locations

paranormal (pair-uh-NOR-muhl)—having to do with an event that has no scientific explanation

psychiatric (si-kee-A-trik)—related to a branch of medicine that studies the mind, emotions, and behavior

quarantine (KWOR-uhn-teen)—to keep a person, animal, or plant away from others to stop a disease from spreading

spirit (SPIHR-it)—a ghost

READ MORE

Hoena, Blake. *Tower of London: A Chilling Interactive Adventure.* You Choose: Haunted Places. North Mankato, Minn.: Capstone Press, 2017.

Pearson, Maggie. *Ghosts and Goblins: Scary Stories from Around the World.* World of Stories. Minneapolis: Darby Creek, 2016.

Peterson, Megan Cooley. *Haunted Hotels Around the World.* It's Haunted! North Mankato, Minn.: Capstone Press, 2017.

INTERNET SITES

Use FactHound to find Internet sites related to this book.

Visit *www.facthound.com*

Just type in 9781543525922 and go.

Check out projects, games and lots more at
www.capstonekids.com

INDEX

Akershus Fortress, 14–15
Ancient Ram Inn, 5–7
Aspairt, Philibert, 27

Black Death, 16
Brown Lady, The, 13

Edinburgh Castle, 24–25
EVP equipment, 6

Gibbons, Mary, 5
Grey Lady, 28, 29

Humphries, John, 6

King Charles II, 21
King Hakon V, 14
King Henry VIII, 22

Langham Hotel, 18–19
ley lines, 7

Malcanisen, 15
Mantelgeisten, 15

Paris Catacombs, 26–27
Poveglia Island, 16–17

Queen Anne Boleyn, 22

Raynham Hall, 12–13
Ruthin Castle Hotel, 28–29

Stonehenge, 7

The Hole, 9, 10, 11
Tower of London, 20–21, 22–23
Townshend, Charles, 12

von Helfenstein, Klara, 8, 9, 10

Walpole, Lady Dorothy, 12–13
Wolfsegg Castle, 8–10
Woman in White, 8, 9
World War II, 14